OVEN DISHES

RECIPE
COOKBOOK

Belongs to

....

....

....

The Oven Dishes is one of the eight cookbooks published as part of a larger collection designed to help you write your own recipes in one place and have them at hand when you cook your favorite meals.

This **Special Collection** also includes:

- **SOUPS**
- **SALADS**
- **PASTRIES**
- **APPETIZERS**
- **DIET RECIPES**
- **VEGAN RECIPES**
- **CAKES AND PIES**

Table of Contents

Recipe	Page

Table of Contents

Recipe	Page

Table of Contents

Recipe	Page

# Table of Contents

Recipe	Page

 # Table of Contents 

Recipe | Page

Recipe:____ 

Prep time:________   Cook time:________   Servings:________

Ingredients	Directions

Notes

Recipe:_______________________________________ 

Prep time:________   Cook time:________   Servings:________

<table>
<tr><td>

Ingredients

</td><td>

Directions

</td></tr>
</table>

Notes

Recipe:

Prep time:______ Cook time:______ Servings:______

Ingredients	Directions

Notes

Recipe:____ 

Prep time:_______   Cook time:_______   Servings:_______

Ingredients	Directions

Notes

Recipe:____ 

Prep time:________   Cook time:________   Servings:________

Ingredients

Directions

Notes

Recipe:____ 

Prep time:________   **Cook time:**________   **Servings:**________

Ingredients

....

....

....

....

....

....

....

....

....

....

....

....

....

....

Directions

....

....

....

....

....

....

....

....

....

....

....

....

....

....

Notes

....

....

....

Recipe:____ 

Prep time:________   Cook time:________   Servings:________

Ingredients

Directions

Notes

Recipe:_______________________________________

Prep time:_______ **Cook time:**_______ **Servings:**_______

Ingredients

Directions

Notes

Recipe:_______________________________________ 

Prep time:________ Cook time:________ Servings:________

Ingredients

Directions

Notes

Recipe:____ 

Prep time:_______   Cook time:_______   Servings:_______

Ingredients	Directions

Notes

Recipe:__________________________________ 

Prep time:_______   Cook time:_______   Servings:_______

Ingredients

Directions

Notes

Recipe:

Prep time:______   Cook time:______   Servings:______

Ingredients

Directions

Notes

Recipe:____ 

Prep time:________   Cook time:________   Servings:________

Ingredients

Directions

Notes

Recipe:_______________________________________

Prep time:_______   Cook time:_______   Servings:_______

Ingredients

Directions

Notes

Recipe:____

Prep time:________   Cook time:________   Servings:________

Ingredients

Directions

Notes

Recipe:____ 

Prep time:_________   Cook time:_________   Servings:_________

Ingredients	Directions

Notes

Recipe:_______________________________

Prep time:_______   Cook time:_______   Servings:_______

<table>
<tr><th>Ingredients</th><th>Directions</th></tr>
</table>

Notes

Recipe:____

Prep time:_______   Cook time:_______   Servings:_______

Ingredients | Directions

Notes

Recipe:_______________________________________ 

Prep time:_______   Cook time:_______   Servings:_______

Ingredients

Directions

Notes

Recipe:____

Prep time:________   Cook time:________   Servings:________

Ingredients

Directions

Notes

Recipe:_______________________________________ 

Prep time:_______   Cook time:_______   Servings:_______

Ingredients	Directions

Notes

Recipe:_______________________________________ 

Prep time:_______   Cook time:_______   Servings:_______

Ingredients

Directions

Notes

Recipe:____ 

Prep time:_______   Cook time:_______   Servings:_______

Ingredients

Directions

Notes

Recipe:

Prep time:______   Cook time:______   Servings:______

Ingredients

Directions

Notes

Recipe:____ 

Prep time:________   Cook time:________   Servings:________

Ingredients

Directions

Notes

Recipe:______________________________________

Prep time:______   **Cook time:**______   **Servings:**______

Ingredients

Directions

Notes

Recipe:____ 

Prep time:_______   Cook time:_______   Servings:_______

Ingredients

Directions

Notes

Recipe:____ 

Prep time:_______   Cook time:_______   Servings:_______

Ingredients

Directions

Notes

Recipe: ____ 

Prep time:_______   Cook time:_______   Servings:_______

Ingredients

Directions

Notes

Recipe:____ 

Prep time:________   Cook time:________   Servings:________

Ingredients	Directions

Notes

Recipe:____ 

Prep time:________   Cook time:________   Servings:________

Ingredients	Directions

Notes

Recipe:________________________________ 

Prep time:________   Cook time:________   Servings:________

Ingredients | Directions

Notes

Recipe:____ 

Prep time:________   Cook time:________   Servings:________

Ingredients

Directions

Notes

Recipe:____ 

Prep time:________   Cook time:________   Servings:________

Ingredients | ## Directions

Notes

Recipe:____ 

Prep time:________   Cook time:________   Servings:________

Ingredients

Directions

Notes

Recipe:____ 

Prep time:________   Cook time:________   Servings:________

Ingredients

Directions

Notes

Recipe:____

Prep time:_______   Cook time:_______   Servings:_______

Ingredients

Directions

Notes

Recipe:____ 

Prep time:________   Cook time:________   Servings:________

Ingredients	Directions

Notes

Recipe:____ 

Prep time:________   Cook time:________   Servings:________

Ingredients	Directions

Notes

Recipe:____ 

Prep time:_______   Cook time:_______   Servings:_______

Ingredients	Directions

Notes

Recipe:____ 

Prep time:________   Cook time:________   Servings:________

Ingredients

Directions

Notes

49

Recipe:____ 

Prep time:________   Cook time:________   Servings:________

Ingredients	Directions

Notes

Recipe:

Prep time:______   Cook time:______   Servings:______

Ingredients	Directions

Notes

Recipe:____ 

Prep time:_______   Cook time:_______   Servings:_______

Ingredients

Directions

Notes

Recipe:____

Prep time:________   Cook time:________   Servings:________

Ingredients

Directions

Notes

Recipe:____

Prep time:________   Cook time:________   Servings:________

Ingredients

Directions

Notes

Recipe:____ 

Prep time:_______   Cook time:_______   Servings:_______

Ingredients

Directions

Notes

Recipe:____ 

Prep time:_______   Cook time:_______   Servings:_______

Ingredients

Directions

Notes

Recipe:____ 

Prep time:________   Cook time:________   Servings:________

Ingredients

Directions

Notes

Recipe: ____ 

Prep time: _______   Cook time: _______   Servings: _______

Ingredients

Directions

Notes

Recipe: ____ 

Prep time: _______   Cook time: _______   Servings: _______

Ingredients

Directions

Notes

Recipe:_______________________________________ 

Prep time:_______ **Cook time:**_______ **Servings:**_______

Ingredients | Directions

Notes

Recipe:____ 

Prep time:_______   Cook time:_______   Servings:_______

Ingredients	Directions

Notes

Recipe:____ 

Prep time:________ Cook time:________ Servings:________

Ingredients

Directions

Notes

Recipe:____ 

Prep time:________   Cook time:________   Servings:________

Ingredients   ## Directions

Notes

Recipe: _______________________________________ 

Prep time: _______   Cook time: _______   Servings: _______

| Ingredients | Directions |

Notes

Recipe:____ 

Prep time:_______   Cook time:_______   Servings:_______

Ingredients

Directions

Notes

Recipe:_______________________________________ 

Prep time:________   Cook time:________   Servings:________

Ingredients

Directions

Notes

Recipe:____ 

Prep time:________   Cook time:________   Servings:________

Ingredients	Directions

Notes

Recipe:_______________________________________ 

Prep time:_______   Cook time:_______   Servings:_______

Ingredients

Directions

Notes

Recipe:____ 

Prep time:________   Cook time:________   Servings:________

Ingredients	Directions

Notes

Recipe:____

Prep time:________ Cook time:________ Servings:________

Ingredients

Directions

Notes

Recipe:____ 

Prep time:_______   Cook time:_______   Servings:_______

Ingredients

Directions

Notes

Recipe:____

Prep time:________   Cook time:________   Servings:________

Ingredients	Directions

Notes

Recipe:____ 

Prep time:_______ Cook time:_______ Servings:_______

Ingredients

Directions

Notes

Recipe:_______________________________________

Prep time:________ Cook time:________ Servings:________

Ingredients	Directions

Notes

Recipe: _______________________________ 

Prep time: _______ **Cook time:** _______ **Servings:** _______

Ingredients

Directions

Notes

Recipe:

Prep time: _______ Cook time: _______ Servings: _______

Ingredients

Directions

Notes

Recipe:____ 

Prep time:________   Cook time:________   Servings:________

Ingredients

Directions

Notes

Recipe:_______________________________________ 

Prep time:________   Cook time:________   Servings:________

Ingredients

Directions

Notes

Recipe:____ 

Prep time:________   Cook time:________   Servings:________

Ingredients

Directions

Notes

Recipe:____ 

Prep time:_______   Cook time:_______   Servings:_______

Ingredients	Directions

Notes

Recipe: _______________________________

Prep time: _______   Cook time: _______   Servings: _______

Ingredients

Directions

Notes

Recipe:_______________________________________ 

Prep time:________   Cook time:________   Servings:________

Ingredients	Directions

Notes

Recipe:____ 

Prep time:________   Cook time:________   Servings:________

Ingredients

Directions

Notes

Recipe:_______________________________________ 

Prep time:_______ Cook time:_______ Servings:_______

Ingredients

Directions

Notes

Recipe:____ 

Prep time:________   Cook time:________   Servings:________

Ingredients	Directions

Notes

Recipe:____

Prep time:_______   Cook time:_______   Servings:_______

Ingredients

Directions

Notes

Recipe:____ 

Prep time:_______   Cook time:_______   Servings:_______

Ingredients

Directions

Notes

Recipe:_______________________________________ 

Prep time:________   Cook time:________   Servings:________

Ingredients	Directions

Notes

Recipe:____

Prep time:________   Cook time:________   Servings:________

Ingredients

Directions

Notes

Recipe:_______________________________________ 

Prep time:________   Cook time:________   Servings:________

Ingredients	Directions

Notes

Recipe:____ 

Prep time:________   Cook time:________   Servings:________

Ingredients	Directions

Notes

Recipe:____

Prep time:________ **Cook time:**________ **Servings:**________

Ingredients	Directions

Notes

Recipe:____ 

Prep time:________   Cook time:________   Servings:________

Ingredients	Directions

Notes

Recipe:_______________________________________

Prep time:_______ Cook time:_______ Servings:_______

Ingredients

Directions

Notes

Recipe:____

Prep time:________   Cook time:________   Servings:________

Ingredients	Directions

Notes

Recipe:_______________________________________ 

Prep time:_______   Cook time:_______   Servings:________

Ingredients	Directions

Notes

Recipe:______________________________________ 

Prep time:______ **Cook time:**______ **Servings:**______

Ingredients

Directions

Notes

Recipe:_______________________________ 

Prep time:_______ Cook time:_______ Servings:_______

Ingredients

Directions

Notes

Recipe:____

Prep time:________   Cook time:________   Servings:________

Ingredients

Directions

Notes

Recipe:_______________________________________ 

Prep time:_______ **Cook time:**_______ **Servings:**_______

Ingredients

Directions

Notes

Recipe:

Prep time: _______   Cook time: _______   Servings: _______

Ingredients | Directions

Notes

Recipe:____ 

Prep time:_______   Cook time:_______   Servings:_______

Ingredients	Directions

Notes

Recipe:____ 

Prep time:_______   Cook time:_______   Servings:_______

Ingredients	Directions

Notes

Recipe:_______________________________________ 

Prep time:_______   Cook time:_______   Servings:_______

Ingredients	Directions

Notes

Recipe:

Prep time: _______   **Cook time:** _______   **Servings:** _______

Ingredients

Directions

Notes

Recipe:____

Prep time:_______ Cook time:_______ Servings:_______

Ingredients

Directions

Notes

Recipe:____

Prep time:_______ Cook time:_______ Servings:_______

Ingredients

Directions

Notes

Recipe:_______________________________________ 

Prep time:________   Cook time:________   Servings:________

Ingredients	Directions

Notes